I'M A GOOD MAN

YOU'RE A GOOD *Woman*

WHY CAN'T WE FIND EACH OTHER?

I'm Ready Publishing
P.O. Box 10254
Houston, TX 77206

Visit our website at www.JeCaryousJohnson.com
Printed in the United States of America

I'M A
GOOD
MAN
YOU'RE A
GOOD
Woman

WHY CAN'T WE FIND
EACH OTHER?

by

JE'CARYOUS JOHNSON

Dedication

This book is dedicated to all the good men and good women who can't seem to find each other, but who never lost the hope or belief they could achieve something remarkable—a fulfilling relationship!

With the deepest gratitude I wish to thank every person who has come into my life and inspired, touched, and illuminated me through their presence. You are the people most responsible for this book. Your questions, concerns, dilemmas, and prayers have been the keys to unlocking the most precious gift of all… the human heart.

For that, I thank you!

Love,

Je'Caryous

Acknowledgements

Wow, God you are so amazing! You have allowed me to wake up every day and live my dreams—dreams of being a blessing to others. You have said, "To whom much is given, much is required." Thank you for making this journey through life an adventure. I hope this book glorifies and magnifies Your name and becomes a roadmap for celestial living.

To my mom, Manon C. Johnson, the queen who brought me into this universe, I can't say thank you enough for supporting me up close and from a distance when I needed space. This book is for you. I have watched you on your never-ending search for a good man. When all else failed, you created what you were looking for in me. Because of you I am the man that I am. God gave me to you as a gift to the world, and He gave you to me so that I may understand the world. In my understanding came a simple truth…this book. May this book and its contents be a blessing to your life and everyone you encounter.

To my sisters, Miracah, Simone, Angela and Frances, I hope this book makes your journey through adulthood a little easier. Stay single until you can choose wisely (smile).

To my father, Frank, thanks for the late-night conversations helping me to understand relationships from a neutral point of view. You have always been there when I needed you and are always willing to help. I am grateful to have you in my life.

Gary Guidry, my partner in crime, thanks for being a marketing genius and a great uncle. Though I am the face of the brand the world must know that the company we share would be handicapped without you.

Ashley Pryor and Jovan Means, my best friends. You have loved me when I have been hard to love. When I have fallen off on the communication you have picked up the pieces. Thank you for your honesty regarding my character and making me always stand for integrity. Thank you for being you.

Dennis, thank you for your friendship and for your endless belief and support of my work. I can say you are one of the most generous people I know. Because of you, I know what friendship really means.

To Charles King and Jay Mandel my agents at William Morris, and Nina Shaw, the best lawyer in the world, thanks for not losing faith in me when times got tough. Let's not forget that every setback was a setup for a comeback. Now, it's our time!

To my fans, you guys are the greatest! We've been together for ten years and counting now. When the world has tried to chastise me, you have encouraged me. I consider you family, and if a man's worth is measured by the love in his family, I am the richest man in the world.

Until next time,
Keep praying, keep loving, keep living, keep playing…

Je'Caryous

Contents

Preface

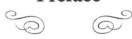

I KNOW THERE ARE GOOD MEN OUT THERE . . . WHY CAN'T I FIND ONE?

It's something I hear all the time from my female relatives, friends, and fans: *Why can't I find a good man? I'm a good woman. It shouldn't be that hard to find a good man.*

In fact, I heard this same sentiment from droves of females responding to an August 2007 article written about me in *Essence* magazine entitled, "More Money, More Problems." It asked a simple question: Why couldn't I, Je'Caryous Johnson, find a woman who wasn't focused on my wallet?

Apparently, many readers did not understand my dilemma, appreciate my answer, nor did they have sympathy for my situation. In fact, there were quite a few angry women who *dared* me to fly them to Houston—first class, of course—so they could show me just how little they cared about my money. Other readers were simply outraged at the audacity I displayed. How dare I not be satisfied with my success alone? They insisted my dilemma was my own fault. These outspoken responses were but a few of the nearly sixty thousand I received. But I must admit, amid the myriad of reactions to the article—

good and bad—there was one general response that forced me to reevaluate my perspective.

A one-lined email from a reader said it best: "There are plenty of good women out here. Why aren't you meeting them?" After a long period of reflection on this statement, I came to a realization. I was asking the wrong question. The true source of my discontent was not the dishonest, deceitful women I seemed to meet at every turn, but the "good," well-intentioned women who—for whatever reason—I did not get to meet at all—or perhaps I did but I didn't recognize it at the time.

I believe there are many men out there just like me— good, decent men whose mothers raised them right and who desire nothing more than a happy, fulfilling, lifelong relationship with a good woman. These men are not part of the status quo—contrary to popular belief, all good men are not dead, gay, or taken. There are many good men in every array of life. We come in all kinds of packages—some of us wear designer suits and sport six-figure incomes while others find our success in jeans working at a car wash, but regardless of our wrapper, we share one commonality, the desire to find a good woman.

Yes, the *Essence* article ignited a firestorm of discussion around me, but it also triggered a deep, introspective conversation within me. As I reflected upon my relationships, I found there were so many questions that I needed to answer, but I had to rewrite, not rephrase, the most important question of all: "I'm a good man, you're a good woman…Why can't we find each other?"

I know I do not ask this question alone. I believe most single men and single women alike desire to find their ideal mate—the "good man" or "good woman" God has created to be their helpmate. This question of why people can't find a companion has led me to write this book.

By no means do I claim to be a psychologist, a psychiatrist, or a therapist. I'm just a good man looking for my good woman, and as a playwright, motivational speaker, and an author, it's a topic that manifests itself quite often. I address it in my plays. I hear it from the fans. I have experienced the frustration myself. Consequently, I decided to explore the matter further.

I started by talking to the ladies of all ages in my life—the platonic friends and the not-so-platonic ones. I examined the relationships where I was wronged and where I was wrong. I talked with every female I encountered, from women on the I'm Ready Productions' message board to ladies at the grocery store. I even developed a survey in hopes of studying the experiences of others. The thousands of respondents—both men and women—are proof this is a hot-button issue close to people's hearts. Of all of the significantly informative data I collected, the most telling truth was the evidence of a lot of people—hurting people—who have all but given up on love.

In the midst of sifting through all of their responses and their feedback, as well as my own personal experiences, this book was born. I've developed reasons why I believe men and women aren't connecting, and I offer real solutions to help us overcome these obstacles.

I'm a Good Man, You're a Good Woman ... Why Can't We Find Each Other? was designed to help you understand the complexities of relationships—not from a professional perspective, but from an everyday person perspective. You'll hear it straight from the sources—good men and good women—who, although their names have been changed, speak candidly on why we're having trouble connecting.

Don't read this book expecting to hear everything a man is doing wrong or all the stuff women should do to catch Mr. Right. It's not a "book of rules", which in fact can cause frustration and confusion, and lead you further from your good man/woman. With this book, I hope to address the real issues that for too long have prevented men and women from truly connecting.

Journey with me as I examine the issues facing most singles today. Hopefully, we will be able to break through the barriers and demolish the obstacles that are preventing good folk from finding one another.

The topics addressed in these pages apply not only to single men and women. Couples in long-term relationships can also benefit from the insight I provide and may even find their relationship stronger as a result.

Define What You Want

Can we be real for a minute? If I asked you what a good man or a good woman looks like, could you tell me? I think one reason good men and women can't find each other is because we don't know what a "good" person looks like. Many women grow up with the notion of a knight in shining armor carrying them away on a white horse into happily ever after.

Once the armor comes off, what does the man look like? I'm not just talking about physically. What qualities does he have mentally, spiritually and emotionally? You may laugh, but this is important. If the man has the body of a Greek god, but the mind of an ant, does that work for you? If he's super-attentive but refuses to set foot in a church, is that okay?

I want you to stop right now, get out a piece of paper and a pen and write down what your ideal mate and your ideal relationship look like.

The Bible says in Habakkuk 2:2 to write the vision and make it plain. You can't go after something if you don't know what it is you're going after.

YOUR LIST MIGHT LOOK SOMETHING LIKE THIS:

- College degree
- No kids
- Christian
- Good looking
- Compatible
- Compliments me often and sincerely

One thing to remember in making your list is that you have to be practical and specific. It's easy to say you want someone to treat you right, but in your list, you have to describe what right looks like to you.

If you require twenty things that a person must have before you will even consider going on a date, there are only a handful of people who will meet the criteria. If, on the other hand, you only have four requirements, you open yourself up to a bigger pool of prospects.

I'm by no means telling you to lower your standards, but I am saying be realistic. Is a college degree a deal breaker for you? For many people it is, which is fine, but there are a bunch of educated fools in the world, and maybe you've let quite a few good people pass you by because they don't have that piece of paper.

Remember your list is just a roadmap. Check it often and change your route if necessary. What matters is that you get to your final destination.

A friend of mine was describing what she wanted in a man. When she finished, I handed her a piece of paper and told her to draw him because that's the closest she'd ever get to that perfect man she was looking for.

You can't demand perfection unless you're offering it.

Let me be clear. There are no perfect men or women out there. You just have to find the one that is perfect for you.

One of the interesting things I've noticed is that as people get older, their list of must-haves gets progressively shorter. A woman in her twenties may have a long list of requirements. But as the years pass and she finds herself still single, the list gets modified. Her no-kids rule that she was adamant about in her twenties just isn't as important in her thirties. Her must-have-a-job rule of her thirties, turned to "oh well, I have my own money" in her forties.

Unlike men, who primarily are drawn to the physical, women tend to look a little deeper. Now, don't get me wrong, women love a good-looking man. I'm reminded of this with every play I write as I have to search for this godlike figure of a man to play the male lead because the women insist on their eye candy. It's just that looks are not the ultimate deciding factor for women like they are for some men.

While the packaging is what initially attracts men, a woman must have additional qualities for a relationship to prosper. The key for both men and women is to clearly identify the things that are really important and why.

"What I'm looking for in a man is confidence," said one of the survey respondents. "He may not be the best-looking man in the room but the way he carries himself makes him the best-looking man in the room. I want a powerful man who knows how to handle an empowered woman. I hate wearing the pants in a relationship. Even though I'm independent, I want someone to come in and take charge of me and make me feel like I'm a woman, even though I'm doing it on my own. I want a man in charge of his life and who is head of the household, who respects me like he respects his mama."

KNOW YOURSELF

Some people are ashamed to admit that among the things they want in a mate is money, or at least financial stability. There is absolutely nothing wrong with that. Seriously, who wants to be with someone who is broke? And there's a difference between broke and building and broke and trifling. The latter has no problem with being broke. The former may have momentarily fallen on hard times, or is at a career building point. That's the kind of person there should be no shame in accepting.

But what's wrong with a woman wanting a man with something? A man wants a woman to be his helpmate but a man that has created no wealth has no worth to a woman because he has not created a world for a woman to be a helpmate in. And a financially secure woman brings more to the table for a goal-oriented man.

Although there are a lot of women who know they are good women and that they want a good man, deep down they don't know what a good man looks like.

While I would love to define what a good man or woman is, there is only one constant. That is the capacity to love. Beyond that you have to know what suits you best.

After years of dealing with trifling men, so many women are afraid to trust their judgment. Some are so busy hopping from one relationship to the next for fear of being alone that they never take the time to examine what they really want.

And after being hurt by one too many women, some men refuse to ever totally commit to anyone. So as they hop from relationship to relationship, he never gives his heart to any one woman.

You must know yourself. What are your passions in life? What are you good at? What are your deal breakers or things you absolutely will not tolerate in a relationship?

I could go on and on, but my point is before you can love anyone else, you have to know and love yourself.

One of the things I really love about the movie *Love and Basketball* was the drive of the main character Monica played by Sanaa Lathan. Monica had been passionate about basketball since she was a little girl, and she didn't apologize for it. Her relationship with her boyfriend, Quincy, played by Omar Epps, was jeopardized by that passion. Even though it took her years, she eventually learned how to make her passion coexist with love. That never would have happened if she didn't know herself.

In order for a good woman and good man to find each other, I urge you to take some time for you. Get to know who you are and what you want, and that way when that good person comes along you'll know it.

DEAL OR NO DEAL

While you have that piece of paper I asked you to get out earlier, I want you to also make a list of your relationship deal breakers. These are the things that you absolutely will not tolerate in any relationship. Do it now before you get into a relationship and your mind gets all cloudy with love—or lust.

For many women, these things are no-brainers—abuse of any kind absolutely will not be tolerated—but for others, it's not so obvious. How do you feel about your man cheating on you? What about addictions of any kind? I just want you to be clear on what acts will have you packing your bags and heading for the door.

I believe another reason why good men and women can't find each other is because we have been in so many bad relationships and ignored so many red flags that we've led ourselves to believe things that really bothered us aren't important. If someone crosses your boundaries—if they do something you can't tolerate—be okay with walking away from that situation. That person might not be good for you.

The bottom line is before you can find a good man or woman you have to be clear on who you are and what you want.

"I always get approached by men who really aren't trying to progress in life. It's like they feel comfortable approaching me, but to be quite honest I've never really been approached by a man who meets my criteria," said one twenty-five-year-old accountant. "Well, my standards are pretty simple: Christian, career driven, family oriented, father material, around my age, respectful, sense of humor, looking to marry, and unselfish. Appearance isn't as important as the personality. Of course, I would prefer a black man who is taller than me with some features I find attractive."

Ken, a handsome, intelligent and very successful physician is looking for a woman that he cannot only be friends with, but one that stimulates him. "I would never be intimidated by a smart, beautiful woman. In fact, I would be proud to call her my woman. I want to be able to look at her and say wow...I've scored! If we are both intelligent, we'll have more to talk about! I can't understand why some men are intimidated to be with a mate that makes just as much money or even more than them. Who cares? As long as the dough's coming in … does it matter from whom?"

"My requests are simple too," added thirty-six-year-old Virginia. "I want a God-fearing, ambitious, family-oriented man with no kids who makes good money, is one hundred percent faithful, comes from a good family, ready to settle down, attractive, romantic, funny, and loves the ground I walk on."

That's simple, right?

Not quite. Many times we're guilty of setting unrealistic expectations. Both men and women create these visions of who they think will be good enough and what he or she will look like and what type of life they will live, etc. These envisioned images are unrealistic. We set our standards so high sometimes that they become unreachable. With standards that high, you'll find yourself by yourself.

WHAT MEN WANT

Studies have shown that needs, wants, and desires can be three of the greatest obstacles in the search for true love. Of course, the essence of what we want, need, or desire is not bad. Instead it is our inability to accept that what we want and desire may not necessarily be what we need.

A question I'm asked all the time by women is what men want. When it comes to finding the perfect mate, men want it all. That may seem a bit generalized, but it's also right on point. Most men really do want their woman to be their everything. In fact, the search for Chaka Khan's "every woman" forces many single men to go through an endless quest for the perfect mate, but what defines perfection? When it comes to relationships, there is no clear-cut definition.

Of the hundreds of men who answered my relationship survey, some common themes prevailed. Men want to be needed; they want to have their basic needs (food, shelter, companionship) met, and they want a woman who is supportive, understanding, and devoted. Additionally, almost every man surveyed was searching for a companion they could trust. Last but not least, nine out of ten of the men surveyed mentioned the need for sexual compatibility.

"I want a woman who has a sexual appetite to match mine," responded Cal, a thirty-two-year-old graphic designer. "I want her to blow my mind while still being able to enrich my mind."

Most of the men surveyed expressed a need to be encouraged and supported. Every man wants to know that no matter what the world may bring, there is someone in his corner who believes he can do no wrong, and when he does make that occasional error, she will still believe in him. Most men want a woman who will support and understand them and not try to change them.

"For me, it's about loyalty," added John, a twenty-eight-year-old survey respondent. "I've got to know a woman has my back. I have to trust that no matter what, she's there for me. That means a lot."

"I need to know if I lose everything tomorrow, will she be gone?" said Kelvin, a thirty-nine-year-old architect.

It all boils down to the four F's—friendship, freedom, fun, and the fantasy, all of which will make a man want a woman to be his fiancée.

Friendship involves getting to know someone without judging them. Freedom simply means knowing you are spending time with someone because you want to. Fun is the enjoyment two people have when they first meet, but it should be maintained throughout the relationship. Finally, fantasy is a result of dressing up and looking good for each other. Men are visual creatures. Although God looks at your heart, men definitely look at the outer appearance.

WHAT WOMEN WANT

I was recently watching the Mel Gibson movie, *What Women Want*. It was a cute concept, and before viewing the movie, I actually chuckled, thinking wouldn't it be great if a man really and truly understood what it is women want. Of course, Hollywood came into play as Gibson so eloquently gained the ability to read women's minds. While entertaining and insightful, the movie was just that—a movie. If only figuring out what women want was as easy as getting a bump on the head.

Since I didn't want to wait around for a concussion to get more insight, I decided to go to the source—the women themselves—to see exactly what it is they want in a man.

I might as well have been asking the women to dissect the Theory of Relativity. The question brought an array of complex answers—at least in my mind. And for the ladies, the checklist was long: true, unadulterated love; trust; honesty; faithfulness; validation; security; caring attitude; understanding; respect; devotion; ambition; and reassurance.

One of my dear friends summed it up simply: A woman wants a man who will treat her right.

It's that definition of right that varies intensely. Right for one woman may be a man who brings home his paycheck and gives his time and money, even though he won't give his heart. For another woman, it may be a man who gives himself completely emotionally, but professionally, there's a lot to be desired.

For my friend Rene, faithfulness was number one on her list. She could deal with murder and mayhem, but she couldn't deal with cheating. For Ashleigh, one of the survey respondents, the man she's looking for has to have a "gift, purpose and passion" and be willing to look at her inner beauty.

One of the most prevailing themes, women said, was finding a man who wasn't intimidated by their success. Men are not intimated by a woman's success per se. They just don't want a woman throwing it in their faces all the time.

Think about it. When a man first sees you he normally knows one thing: that you're beautiful. He doesn't have a clue about your bank account or your degrees until you tell him. If you feel your success is keeping you from finding a good man, keep that information to yourself until you see where the relationship is headed.

"But won't he realize I'm successful when he sees my BMW?" you ask.

Maybe, but there are plenty of people driving BMWs who can't afford them. If the man you're dating is more drawn to your BMW and your bank account than your brains and beauty, chances are high this isn't the good man you've been waiting for.

Let me be clear that I have no problems with a woman being successful. I do have a problem when it comes at the expense of everything and everyone else. I believe there are a lot of men—and women—who feel like I do.

Success is not going to keep you warm at night. Like Billy

Dee Williams said in the movie *Mahogany*, "Success is nothing without someone you love to share it with."

What it comes down to is figuring out your definition of right, which hopefully you have a clearer understanding of since you've made your list of qualities of a good man or good woman and your list of deal breakers. It's cool to say you want to be treated right, but until you know what is right for you, you are fighting a losing battle in finding your good man or woman.

So now that you have defined what you want and have a general overview of what men and women in general want, let's get to the real reason you're reading this book: the obstacles that are keeping you from finding each other.

Obstacle 1:
Forces of Attraction

This discussion would not be complete—or honest—without a mention of the first thing that catches a man's eye, a woman's appearance. Among the list of wants submitted during my relationship survey, almost every man mentioned one of the following: a flattering figure, manicured nails, well-styled hair, or an attractive smile. Simply said, most men are visual creatures, and the decision to approach a woman is often made at first sight. It's been happening since the beginning of time. When God presented Eve to Adam, the first thing he noticed was her beauty. Yes, this assessment is superficial, but it is also essential in a man's selection of a mate.

I'm going to be real with you. Most men won't verbally admit it, but the physical attributes of a woman top the proverbial male wish list. Every man wants a beautiful woman. Please allow me to define the word *beauty*.

While there are more than ten different definitions of beauty listed in any given dictionary, when it comes to the physical beauty of people, each of us has our own definition. It is true that some men are easily captivated by the images of beauty we see every day on TV and in magazines, however, many of us actually search for something different, more unique. Beauty truly is a personal preference. This initial attraction is very important. If a man is not physically attracted to a woman, it is highly improbable he will approach her with any romantic intentions.

However, I'm not going to disregard those instances in which some men become involved in a relationship with a woman they did not initially find attractive. In fact, these relationships are extremely important because they prove that the male heart is connected to more than just his eyes (and his libido). Physical beauty only ranks first because this assessment takes place first. There are many other measures that are far more important when it comes to what a man really wants.

CONVERSATION

Once a man finds himself physically attracted to a woman and the initial contact is made, a conversation ensues. Conversation is key. If it's not there, most men will walk away, no matter how beautiful the woman is— unless, of course, he's just interested in having a potential sex partner, not a potential life partner. For a man to really consider you for a long-term relationship, he must be able to talk to you. He must feel empowered by you and not condemned.

The movie *Jerry Maguire* is the perfect example of this. Although the main character played by Tom Cruise was not initially attracted to love interest Renee Zellweger, her conversation and unwavering support of him eventually won him over. When things started getting rocky in their relationship, conversation is part of what brought him back to her. She said, "You had me at hello," following his heartfelt plea to take him back because she recognized that just the act of showing up demonstrated the depth of his commitment.

A real-life example is survey respondent Kevin. He recently dumped his plain-Jane girlfriend for a beautiful, supermodel type with legs from here to eternity. In fact, all of his friends thought he'd won the lottery, and they vehemently gave him major props for "hooking up with a dime like that."

Kevin loved being envied, but after a month he realized he missed the conversation, the affection, the attention, and everything else he'd gotten from that plain- Jane girlfriend.

"I couldn't even hold a conversation with her," Kevin lamented of the supermodel type. "She was the center of every conversation. I asked her what she thought about Barack Obama's winning the presidency; she said it was 'cool.' She actually said that she had not even bothered to vote because her vote didn't count. Then she proceeded to talk about whether she should wear her hair up or down for the weekend event we had to attend. After a while stuff like that gets old—real old."

After the physical attraction wanes or wears out, there has to be something else to sustain the relationship, so men look for strong conversation and compatibility during those early interactions. Is she smart? Is she kind? Caring? Humble? Does she treat him well? Will she be there for him no matter what?

There are any number of questions a man may ask himself during this stage of the relationship assessment. At this point his list of wants may change. The woman may have met his original list of requirements, but he still finds himself unsatisfied, or maybe he discovers something in his partner he never realized he wanted. This stage of assessment and evaluation is critical as it often determines the progression, success, or failure of a relationship.

COMMON INTERESTS AND GOALS

It doesn't take long before the relationship moves beyond looks and conversation. In order to find your good man or woman, you've got to have common interests and goals. Men and women want the object of their interest to possess enough characteristics on their wish list that they don't need to look for or date anyone else to have those needs met. Again, these needs vary from person to person.

I'm not saying you have to like everything your man or woman does, but you do need to have some things in common so when the rough times come—and they will come—you have a foundation. Beyond the common interests and goals, you both have to desire the same things if your relationship has a true chance of succeeding.

Aren't these pretty much the same things women desire? At the end of the day, we all want to be loved and needed. We want someone's eyes to light up when we enter a room.

Here are a few responses from men who took my survey about what attracts them to a woman beyond the physical.

Phil, a first-year law student, is constantly meeting women who are excited about the man he is going to become. "I am always seen as the guy with so much potential. They're looking at what they can mold me into. I'm looking for a woman who accepts and supports who I am right now."

Some other common themes the surveyed men look for in a committed relationship include appreciation and admiration.

"Women hear admiration and they automatically think 'oh, you want somebody to jock you,'" says Calvin, a thirty-five-year-old stockbroker. "That's not it at all. I want a woman who is proud of me. Call me arrogant if you want, but I want to feel like I'm her superhero/knight in shining armor/Prince Charming."

In this age of independent women, personally, I'm looking for a woman who is independently dependent. She _can_ do for herself if she has to but she has no problem depending on me. If she doesn't need me for anything, why am I even there?

I remember dating a girl who didn't hesitate to let me know she didn't need me to do, and I quote, "a damn thing" for her. She made her own money, took care of her own house, mowed her own lawn, changed her own flat tire, etc. All I could think was, *What do you need me for then? Can you mow my lawn, too?*

I'm not alone. Men want to feel needed. Ladies, even if you feel like you don't need a man, at least act like you do. Call it egotistical or whatever, but the bottom line remains, a man wants to feel like he adds something to your life.

Once the physical attraction wears off, some men want the extreme—the completely dependent woman.

"Call me old fashioned but I still want a woman who wants to stay at home and depends on me to keep things going. I want someone who likes cleaning the house, caring for the kids, and cooking dinner. But it's getting harder and harder to find that," said Julian, a thirty-three-year-old accountant.

For the most part, men want a balance. Not completely dependent, but not wholly independent. A man wants to be his woman's superhero. We are bred to be the breadwinner, provider, protector (physically and emotionally). A woman is born of man's rib (obviously God used the best rib man had to create her), therefore, man is walking around incomplete until he finds the best part of him. Hence the phrase from *Jerry Maguire, You complete me.* Women represent what embodies that man, what he stands for, the best parts of him. That is why it says in Proverbs 18:22, "He that findeth a wife findeth a good thing."

SUPPORTIVE ENVIRONMENT

I'm sure a lot of women will agree, many men want the cake, icing, *and* the plate. I believe that's true. Most men want the virtuous woman described in Proverbs 31 who desires to take care of her family to the best of her ability all the days of her life. We want a woman who is not only beautiful but one who has our back. If you're independent, then use your education and money as my secret weapon. Don't use it to replace or belittle me. For most successful men, if their woman is working, it's because she wants to. If a man is poor and lands a job making good money, the chances are high he's going to shower his woman with gifts.

For survey respondent Charles, it's an issue of encouragement.

"I'm going to make mistakes. I want a woman who builds me up and not tears me down. I have a hard enough time out there in the real world. I don't want to come home and have my woman beating me down as well. I had a woman go off when I made a bad decision to leave my job and venture out on my own. When it didn't work out she proceeded to tell me how stupid I was to leave such a great-paying job for a pipe dream. Needless to say we're no longer together."

SEX VS. INTIMACY

Since we're being honest, I'll tell you if most men could have more than one woman, or at least if they could be physically involved with more than one woman, with no consequences, they would. Emotionally, now that's a different story.

"It's hard enough trying to stay emotionally connected to one woman," said forty-one-year-old Luke. "I can't imagine trying to juggle and meet the emotional needs of more than one woman, but straight sex, with no attachments, that's an idea I could get with."

Most women can't understand this, but men can have sex with no emotional attachments. It has nothing to do with a woman's looks, contrary to popular belief. We are external creatures, women are internal. Even our sexual parts are reflective of that. A man enters a woman, thus a woman can become emotional being with that man because he has entered her essence and she has made him a part of her.

Many women make the mistake of thinking men are primarily driven by sex alone and think if they can attract a man sexually, they will be able to attract him emotionally as well.

Women too often give up sex to a man in the hopes it will translate into a relationship and get them what they want—a good man. In reality, a man has the capacity to view a sexual connection and an emotional connection as two entirely different things, and it requires a special set of skills to mold these two things together and keep them connected in a man's mind.

While it might not seem like it, most men are looking for more than just sex. There are so many women who believe sex entitles them to half a man's empire.

A woman who knows how to fulfill a man emotionally and sexually will be the woman who captures a man's heart and gets that same fulfillment for herself. He will roll over one day and in an instant look at that woman who fulfills him and say, "I want to feel like this for the rest of my life." This is when a man realizes he's found his good woman and asks her to marry him.

The problem is as soon as they are engaged the man and woman are going full steam ahead in two different directions. She's planning the wedding, and he just wants to keep the honeymoon-type behavior going that got him to the place of proposing in the first place.

Basically, men want the same thing as women—love. It's our understanding of how to reach that destination that seems to be the problem.

At the end of the day, don't get caught up in the superficial, which I believe success and beauty to be. Beauty might be what catches a man's eye, but it's your other qualities that are going to reel your good man in and keep him coming back for more.

DIVERSITY

The idea of perfection varies from person to person. As my grandmother used to say, "There is a lid for every pot." Truer words have rarely been spoken. Diversity is the spice of life. The fact that we yearn for something different in our mate is the very thing that gives each of us a chance at real love.

My friends and their description of their perfect woman are good examples of diversity. We have had many discussions about women and settling down. While some want to get married sooner than others, almost all of us are willing to admit we eventually hope to find that one person who is perfect for us.

Now, while the guys in my inner circle and I may occasionally find ourselves sharing similar thoughts over the same woman in a social setting or at a group function, the similarities in what we truly want in a mate stop there. The women we have actually dated are all very different just like all of us are different.

For example, Mark is an old-fashioned traditionalist. The woman he marries must be prepared to love, honor, and obey. He wants to be the breadwinner, the decision maker, and the proverbial head of the household. Consequently, he prefers to date women who are not consumed with their career, but instead, Mark searches for a woman who is eager and able to make him her top priority. He proclaims, "I need to be number one."

A serial monogamist, Mark expects a lot from the women he dates, but he also demands a lot of himself. He fully commits himself to every relationship. He is a protector and a provider. None of his girlfriends have ever complained of being neglected or unappreciated. Instead, Mark has worked hard to build and strengthen his financial portfolio so he can dedicate the time and the money it will take to develop the relationship he desires.

Will, on the other hand, is very different. He is divorced and prefers an independent woman, someone who is career-driven and focused. Additionally, she cannot require a lot of time or attention. She should have her own life, her own friends, and her own activities. More importantly, she must allow Will to have the same, and rarely should their two worlds encroach upon each other. Will needs his space—lots of space.

Will is a successful businessman and an avid golfer. Much of his business is done on the golf course, and over the years he has developed a true passion for the game. He hits a round of golf almost every weekend, and any woman he is dating should not only be prepared, but understanding of this.

While Will sounds incorrigible, he is very open-minded and supportive. He has no issue dating women who earn more money or achieve greater success than he does. Will is most attracted to the woman who is the life of the party, the center of attention. He does not gravitate toward wallflowers. The successes in Will's last two relationships were due to the fact that he dated a doctor and an actress, both of whom loved the way their hectic schedules and exciting lifestyles were a complement to his.

And then there's Louis, who is unsure of what he wants. A self-proclaimed sucker for love, he approaches every potential partner with a hope she might be "the one." Consequently, this hopeless romantic has experienced more than his fair share of heartbreak and rejection. He's been engaged three times.

Despite his hard lessons in love, the lifelong marriages of both Louis' parents and grandparents serve as inspirational examples to him of what can be. In fact, it is these relationships that have driven Louis into this passionate and painful search for unconditional love and happily ever after.

Louis wants the helpmate described in Proverbs 31, and in an effort to find her, he works hard to be what he believes every woman wants. He describes himself as "romantic, sensitive, chivalrous, and a [great] listener." Contrary to this self-description, he is not weak-willed or timid. Louis is a good guy, and he is determined to do whatever it takes to be a good husband, and eventually, a good father.

Lastly is James, the infamous player. He boldly proclaims he is not now, nor is he ever going to get married. "The male-to-female ratio just leans too much in a brother's favor. Twenty to one, man, twenty to one." James' only want in a woman is that she is a woman. He does not discriminate.

At thirty-two years old, James still hits the club, the bar, or the newest social hot spot at least three nights a week. He also continues to keep count of the amount of phone numbers he's collected at the end of the night. There are always more than a few.

Now most people would assume sensible women would spot James from a mile away and head in the other direction, but that is not reality. A former pro athlete, many women approach him. Whatever attracts the ladies to him does not compare to what keeps them coming back: his personality. James has never met a stranger. Everyone who speaks to him is his friend, and he does an incredible job of remembering names and faces.

James is also outgoing and hilarious. Many women discover that hanging with him is anything but boring. They also discover they are rarely the only woman vying for James' attention. Some women are okay with sharing, but many others approach him in hopes they will be the one to change him. Many have tried; all have failed. The countless attempts to settle him have proven unsuccessful, but maybe one day…

As for me, I usually love an intelligent, confident, driven woman. To me, lots of beauty plus no brains equals no good. I need a gracious woman who is humble and all about serving others. It goes without saying that she has to be a Christian and she has to realize the importance of family.

My mother raised me to be the good man she could never find, and I know how to treat a woman. Unfortunately, I find that I am more often a giver and rarely a recipient of the things that I require in a relationship.

I've come to realize that I've been guilty of expecting the women I've dated to be like me in their thinking and needs. I would question a woman's love if she reacted and behaved in ways that were contrary to what I believed. Finally, after experiencing a few disappointments, it occurred to me that men and women both give the kind of love they desire.

Some women I have dated have complained I pull away when something is bothering me. Finally, I had to explain to one girlfriend that I have a fear of not being good enough or incompetent, so I compensate for it by focusing on being successful. It scares me to think I am supposed to be the breadwinner in the house, especially if I don't feel as though I'm bringing in the bread. My ex-girlfriend just didn't get this, until I explained a man not being able to provide is just as devastating to him as a woman not being able to conceive and give birth. It's a huge blow to our manhood.

All men have their own cross to bear. As displayed in the fairly comprehensive descriptions of my friends, single men have a very diverse list of wants. If asked, most of my friends would also say that their wants and desires directly align with their needs. I, and most of the male survey respondents, tend to disagree. According to the answers of the men surveyed online, their wants in a good woman varied just as drastically as my friends'. However, there were some very consistent themes that ran throughout all of the male responses that lead me to believe that all men *need* the same thing.

First, almost every man surveyed mentioned in some form or another, the *need* to be needed. None of the men surveyed, and none of my friends for that matter, ever expressed a desire to be a piece of artwork; a present, inanimate object that serves no intrinsic purpose, except to occasionally be looked at lovingly. Instead they all expressed the need to be an irreplaceable part of a woman's life. I feel I need to make a positive difference.

Now, please don't misunderstand. Most men appreciate an independent woman—a woman who has pursued and accomplished great success in her education and career. Still, while we know deep down it is not true, most men also like to believe that these same women have a pantry filled with unopened pickle jars just waiting on a good man to swoop in and save the day by opening them.

I recently attended a dinner party at the home of a good friend. Naturally, the course of conversation moved toward relationships. One young woman spoke candidly about her experiences with men. Very accomplished, this young woman has earned numerous degrees and advanced to great heights in her career; however, she said that she often finds men are intimidated by her success. A male dinner party attendee responded best, saying she must be meeting the wrong men. Additionally, he said that he is never intimidated by women. Instead, in his relationships he tries to fit into a place in the woman's life where he is needed. "Most independent women go out of their way to prove that they do not need a man. You don't need a man to open your door, carry your bag, change your tire, or give an opinion on anything. If I am not needed, why I am there?"

Obstacle 2:
Fear

Let me start off by assuring you that I am not going to be talking about fear of commitment. While there are many men who are afraid of this, what I want to discuss is a fear of being taken advantage of, something that affects both men and women.

A few of you might be rolling your eyes, but hopefully what I'm about to share drives home my point.

A few years ago I was on a date with a woman in Miami when I received a call from my stockbroker. I had been waiting on that call all week and decided to take it. I asked her to excuse me while I took the call. During the brief conversation, I told the broker to sell twenty thousand shares. After I hung up, my date eagerly asked how much money my twenty thousand shares equaled. I was a little hesitant but answered her question. "Two hundred thousand dollars," I replied.

I swear, it was like the cartoons, where dollar signs appeared in her eyes.

"For that amount of money, I could lease a Bentley or get a pair of Chanel shoes for every day of the week," she said, adding she couldn't be with a man who wasn't willing to buy her things. "I live a certain way. I expect certain things," she said.

Dates like that soon became the story of my life. I've been in the entertainment industry for over ten years, and the more success I achieve, the more gold diggers cross my path. When I mentioned my dilemma in the *Essence* magazine article, I talked about that Miami date and how this woman tried to make me her next "victim."

Boy, the ladies let me have it. I was immediately blasted by people who wrote in saying things like, "Maybe if you weren't walking around sporting a fifteen-thousand-dollar Rolex, women wouldn't try to date you for your money." Still others said I attracted gold-digging women because I looked like a miner on a quest for gold. True, I want a gold mine, but do I have to dress down, hide the kind of car I drive, or portray myself to be something I'm really not, to achieve that goal? I was raised to take care of women, so in my mind I was handling my responsibilities. When I showered a woman with gifts, I was truly doing it out of the goodness of my heart.

But now, I wonder if I should do like one of my friends. He comes from old money—I'm not talking rich, he's super-wealthy. Though he has a Lamborghini, a high-rise condo, and money for generations, he also has a small, beat-up pickup truck, a raggedy apartment, and he worked part-time at

Continental Airlines (yeah, I know it's crazy but he gets free flying benefits). My friend did all of this because he said he was tired of attracting women who saw only the bling. He felt by portraying himself one way, he could attract a woman who saw him for him and not his money, and he wouldn't have to fear losing his heart to a woman who wasn't there because she genuinely wanted to be with him and not his money.

Yes, there were many, many, many women who didn't give him the time of day. When he found one who did, who he really liked, she dumped him when he broke the news that he was rich because she felt like he'd been deceitful. He's still working to get her back.

Is it really necessary to do all of that, just to attract the right woman?

I think not.

The dating game is scary. Many people are afraid to put their hearts on the line out of fear of someone taking advantage of them. Repeatedly we are told in the Bible to fear not. Even if you don't admit it to anyone but yourself, deep down, don't you fear meeting someone, putting your heart out there only to have it stepped on? Exposing yourself to someone is a huge risk. There are no guarantees in any relationship.

No one can really tell you how to prevent having your heart broken. There is one fact: If you don't put your heart on the line for anyone, you will go through life and have never loved anyone. That in itself provides barriers that can be insurmountable.

There are people who take that fear to the extreme, jumping to conclusions after only a few minutes of meeting someone.

"I was really feeling this one woman," says twenty-nine-year-old Jay. "But it was obvious the feelings weren't reciprocated. It took me about three weeks to find out why, and I was floored when a mutual friend told me it was because of my shoes. She made a decision in an instant because she said my shoes looked cheap."

Jay considers himself lucky he didn't get with that woman, but considering the fact that he makes six figures (he just hates shopping) and he is a firm believer in fidelity and treating his woman like a queen, Jay says she is the one who missed out.

This woman was a victim of fear.

Fear kept her from giving my friend a fair chance. In essence, she broke up with him before he could break up with her.

Have you ever been guilty of this?

Are you so afraid of being hurt that fear is strangling the life out of your new relationships before they can begin?

Whenever you're in a situation where you are dismissing people based on something as trivial as what they have on, realize there is something deeper at work. I believe it's fear—whether it's fear of what your friends will say or fear that a man won't provide for you—realize it for what it is and work to overcome it.

Remember, fear is **f**alse **e**vidence **a**ppearing **r**eal. Look at the reality of your situation, and know ninety percent of what we fear never happens. If you dated a great guy whose only issue was his shoes, the reality is he can get new shoes. If you're worried about what your friends will say, wouldn't your true friends be happy you've found your good man, regardless of the package he's dressed in?

My advice is to stop operating out of fear and instead step out on faith.

Obstacle 3: Communication

A friend of mine recently came to me distraught because he'd just found out his girlfriend was pregnant. They were both struggling financially. He already had two kids and had no plans on having another. He did use protection, but of course, that's not foolproof, as evidenced by the bombshell his girlfriend dropped on him.

Because they had talked about how neither of them were ready for kids, and she'd told him she wasn't against abortion, he just assumed they'd get the situation handled.

Most people are afraid to discuss their past, and it becomes one of the main complications in building a future.

But because they were so busy basking in the glow of a new relationship, they never really talked. I mean, *really* talked. If they had, he would've learned she'd had an abortion when she was twenty-one that had almost killed her physically and emotionally.

My friend didn't understand because after all, his girl had said she wasn't against abortions, and she wasn't—as long as it was someone else. The part they didn't talk about was her being against having an abortion herself.

They both admit that they glossed over the issue because it was "too deep" and they enjoyed keeping things lighthearted.

That's a prime example of how serious issues can get lost in translation without proper communication.

The ability to effectively communicate is something both men and women said they wanted in a mate, but that phrase, *ability to effectively communicate,* goes much deeper than it sounds. Men and women simply don't see things the same, and that breakdown in communication leads to tremendous roadblocks.

Hence, the success of the book *Men are from Mars, Women are from Venus.* The author, John Gray, built a lucrative franchise on the simple concept that men and women see things differently.

A lot of the issues men and women have with each other, as I mentioned earlier, happen due to miscommunication ("I thought you said" or "I thought you meant"). It's something forty-four-year-old Donna knows all too well.

"That would probably be the biggest problem I have with my husband. We were both communication majors in college, but it's like we can't talk to each other," she said. "If I tell him to make a right at the stoplight, he'll swear I said make a left at the stop sign."

I agree with John Gray, men and women speak different languages. It's as though men speak Greek and women speak French. The fact that they speak different languages isn't the issue. The problem comes when women spend all of their time learning to speak Greek. This allows them to communicate with men, but men never learn to speak French, so they still aren't effectively communicating. No matter how much you desire to communicate with your mate, know you can't do it alone. It's a two-way street.

For men, a lot of communication has to do with desire. They simply don't want to get into deep conversations that oftentimes, many think will lead to an argument they can't win or into territory they'd rather not venture. The most dreaded phrase a man can hear is, "We need to talk." Men have the patience to sit and watch a game for hours but can't communicate with his woman for five minutes. Communication is crucial to any successful relationship and has led to the downfall of many "good" relationships. Keep in mind, what you do say is just as important as what you don't. That nonverbal communication can also make or break a relationship.

Tammy, a fifty-year-old survey respondent, shared this story:

One friend in particular kept having the same problems with women. His response was "I'm tired of this. It's always the same ol', same ol'." I watched him as he ventured into a new relationship and then the complaining began again. I started to ask him some probing questions, and based on his answers, I provided him with a detailed description of how the woman responded. He was amazed at my insight. We discovered he was someone who said he wanted to take it slow before developing a relationship, but he gave all his time to this woman and absorbed her time as if he were in a relationship. When he felt they were getting too close he wanted to back up, but she had taken all her time away from her other relationships (friends, family, dating others), devoted herself to him, thereby keeping the relationship tone, not realizing he was backing up. He was upset she wouldn't back up as quickly as he did and called it the same ol', same ol' when it came to women.

Then I informed him, you're getting the same ol', same ol' because you are sending mixed messages to the women with whom you interact.

Tammy's story is one that so many men and women live. A lot of times, women respond to men's behavior. They'll take his lead and adjust to what he's doing, not necessarily what he is saying.

Men will say we are not in a relationship, but we don't want you dating anyone else.

By nature, men are not emotional creatures, and therefore, for the most part, it is hard for women to decipher what men think and how they feel. That's where a lot of women go wrong. The preventative measure? Men need to open up and communicate. Let your actions back up your words, then there won't be any confusion as to what's really in your heart.

I can't stress the importance of talking about everything, not just the stuff on page one of the dating manual. What if I like playing basketball on Fridays and she likes skating? Well, in the beginning I may go skating because I'm trying to impress her, but ultimately I'll start to feel some resentment. If there's ever a time when you need to be honest in your communication, it's in the beginning stages of a relationship. If you get to know each other in the beginning, in an honest and open manner, then the person is given the opportunity to express his or her flaws and mistakes without judgment.

A woman has to trust you to love you, but a man has to love you to trust you.

In the beginning of relationships, people try to appease their mate. As the relationship progresses people lose that desire along the way. It's the same feeling as when you purchase a new car. You drive it all the time, you love it. Then it gets old and you don't spend as much time in it anymore. It's crucial to find that balance.

Obstacle 4:
Baggage

When my friend was engaged, he and his fiancée were having problems and she kept running to a book instead of listening to what he needed. He eventually asked, "Am I going to have to write a book for you to listen to me?" She was insulted. He was pissed. Needless to say they never got married. I often thought about why they were engaged in the first place. He soon realized he was grieving from the death of his grandmother. His fiancée was still dealing with the sudden death of her mother. Her mother's birthday and his birthday were a day apart. Death can make you reevaluate life. When it was all said and done, he and his fiancée were both two grieving people who found comfort in each other but not love. They failed to unpack their bags, and their relationship suffered because of it.

As difficult as it may be, when you get in a new relationship, it is important to unpack your bags. How can you truly give your all to a new relationship if you're still clinging to the old one?

I have this theory I call Pebble in the Prada. If a woman is walking around with a pebble in her Prada shoe, she can only ignore it for so long. If she leaves it in there long enough, one day she's going to wake up and realize her foot is permanently damaged. Many people ignore the pebbles in their relationships for too long only to wake up one day and realize they are permanently damaged.

Meeting a good man or good woman isn't the hard part. The hard part is making it work. The more your relationship grows, the more complicated it gets. The last thing you need is what so many of us carry—emotional baggage from a past relationship. Think of it this way: When you're traveling, overweight luggage always costs more. There is a high cost to pay for emotional baggage as well. Not letting go may result in a problematic and unsuccessful relationship. Carrying that baggage can often leave you stuck on the tarmac. Relationships cannot move forward or take off because of refusal to let go of past hurts and latent insecurities.

FORGIVE AND FORGET

Sometimes, you may even need to unpack some things in your own relationship—drama you've gone through that you're trying to work past. You may need to empty out your lockbox—the place where men and women guard their feelings of insecurities, previous hurts, etc.

Unfortunately, many of us never forget a betrayal. We are just waiting for the opportunity to bring it up again.

One of my former coworkers has what I call a mental Rolodex. Whenever her man messes up, she files the act away in that Rolodex and as soon as they get into an argument, she pulls it out and throws it back in his face.

When a man says I'm sorry for a mistake he made and you say you forgive him, you must really forgive him and not bring it up anymore. No one wants to continue to pay for past mistakes.

FEAR REVISITED

When a woman feels insecure about her relationship, she will tend to pull back. If a woman thought the relationship was going somewhere and then realizes it's not, she will move around or find a plan B. Women often have an exit strategy.

But be careful. Don't move on to the next man if you are still not finished getting over the last one. When you fail to unpack your bags, you are getting into something that will deeply hurt you. It will hurt the people you love. Some of life's biggest, most devastating mistakes have been made for love, or what appeared to be love. This emotional baggage leads to something we've already discussed: fear.

I know some people who have this fear of committing

to a relationship because past experience has them thinking the bottom may drop out or they're just fearful that things are moving too fast. That fear often leads to sabotage.

When you are dating someone, people take each other as is. We are all used goods in some way. Life itself takes the innocence away, but for however long or brief the dating period, things are great. I'm not talking about when you start to claim each other because that's when it gets complicated. As soon as you put a title on what you have, it is like putting a barbwire fence around your property. The only problem is you think you are putting this fence or title on the person you're with to keep other people away.

What you end up doing is making the person you're with feel trapped. The relationship is no longer fun anymore. Now a man starts to feel like he has lost who he is and doesn't like who he has become, so he goes back to the only thing he knows to get control of his life and his freedom again—cut a hole out of the fence and sneak out.

Even though he repairs it, he will never fix the fence the way it should be because he would be trapping himself all over again, so he repairs it just enough to keep sneaking out every now and then. Then, it is just a matter of time before that woman discovers he has been leaving the yard.

"Good women who have had their share of bad relationships are on guard waiting for the axe to drop because we know it's coming," said one female survey respondent. "There will be some children you weren't aware he had or the expectation that you will be a babysitter for his child or the overly aggressive baby mama or financial problems."

The most important thing is recognizing you do indeed need to unpack.

"I believe I still need to heal from my last relationship," she continued. "Every man I meet, I scare him away because I don't give him a chance. I think everything he says is a lie because I have flashbacks on what I went through. I am not emotionally ready to be in a relationship. I have to learn how to love me again first before I can accept a new man in my life. I have to learn how to be happy and satisfied with me first."

THE TIES THAT BIND

If your issues are rooted deeper than a male-female relationship, recognize that, too, and don't be afraid to get counseling to get yourself right first.

"My biological father abandoned me as a child," said thirty-four-year-old Debbie. "My mother remarried (she celebrated twenty-six years this year), and I have a wonderful father, but I always feel as if I wasn't good enough for the first man in my life. Why should I be good enough for any other man?"

You may have to unpack and leave all those family members, well-meaning friends, haters, blockers, and others, all of which can cause major issues outside of your relationship.

"I had to learn to stop talking about my relationship with my girls," said Shida, a thirty-three-year-old journalist, "because long after I forgave him, my girls were still looking at him sideways. So while they meant well, ultimately, it got to the point they didn't have anything positive to say about him."

Most relationships are successful because outsiders and their thoughts/suggestions/comments/relationship advice are not asked for or accepted by most of the aforementioned people.

There's no way you can completely purge yourself of past pains, but learn from the good and bad of those relationships that didn't work, and when it's time to move on, unpack and take along only the good.

READ THE SIGNS

According to Match.com, an online dating website, there are ways to know when you're ready to move on.

1. **Your ex's name is not always coming out of your mouth.** You might need to talk about the person when you first break up to help you process it all, but if it's been six months and every other sentence includes his name, you haven't let go yet.

2. **You've erased signs of him.** The ticket stub to the Frankie Beverly and Maze concert should not still be stuck in the corner of your mirror, and you should have deleted all the sweet voice mails that remind you of what used to be.

3. **Reminders should not hurt your heart.** If you're truly over your ex, watching his favorite team play may make you nostalgic for a second, but it shouldn't last for days.

4. **You're happy he's happy.** If you find out your ex is dating someone else, it may make you jealous initially, but you shouldn't lose sleep over it.

5. **Stop comparing.** You should not compare each new person you date to your ex. If you have a bad date, be okay with it being bad and having nothing to do with your ex.

6. **Being alone is okay.** If you dread the nights or weekends because all you can think about is being alone, that's a sign you haven't moved on. There will come a day when you're okay with being alone, and that's when you're more likely to find someone.

Obstacle 5:
Looking for Love in All the Wrong Places

I met a woman in a nightclub once and after buying her a drink and talking for a little while, she came straight out and told me she was looking for Mr. Right. I stared at her dumbfounded, before saying, "And you think you're going to find him in a nightclub?"

Take it, I was at the same club but I wasn't looking for Mrs. Right, I was more interested in Ms. Right Now!

One of the biggest challenges of dating is trying to figure out where to go to find single men and women who are educated, career driven, or simply heading in the right direction. Be honest. How many of you are tired of the club scene? You want to meet the man or woman of your dreams, but you don't go anywhere or do anything to make that happen. It's almost as if you think your soul mate will show up on your front door.

It is my belief that to find your perfect mate you must go on your own journey in life. Go do what it is that you are meant to do and you will find him or her walking down the same road as you. A football coach loves football, therefore it is likely he will meet his woman at an event associated with what it is he loves. If a football coach marries a woman who hates football, divorce is likely because it is just a matter of time before the very game he loves becomes a conflict for the woman he loves.

I know some people are too impatient to wait for fate to step in, so to find your good man or woman, go to the places that match the qualities for which you're looking. If you want a Christian, go to church; if you want a handyman, go to Home Depot. If looks are important, hang out near a beauty or barbershop or nail salon. It is my belief that you will naturally hang out in places that you love and it is in those places where you will find like-minded people.

Also, in this age of technology, don't rule out the Internet. If you are like me and you're always online, why not consider looking for love there? More and more often, I am hearing stories of people finding true love on social media sites like Facebook and MySpace as well as websites like eharmony.com and match.com. Some of these sites charge a fee to join, but how is that any different from a cover charge you would pay to go to a club? Don't let the costs hinder you from being exposed to a wider pool of people.

There might be a few of you who are a little worried about this idea, but these sites don't have the stigma they once did. A long time ago, people were worried about who exactly they were encountering. Sometimes people would post pictures that were ten years old and post information that was not true, but I think that's changed. Now thanks to cell phones, you can take a picture in an instant and post it, which many people do, and I believe people are being more honest too.

There are more people looking for love online than you think. As with anything, I urge you to do your homework with someone you meet on the Internet, just like you would with someone you meet in person.

MISSING THE MARK

There are so many reasons why good men and women don't connect. Here's a sampling of opinions.

From Miguel: "The reason people can't find each other is because they are all looking for the wrong things in all the wrong places. They want true love but they are seeking big bank accounts, big penises, good looks, and bling. Those are not the qualities of true love. True love isn't flashy and loud. It is quiet, caring, and shared with someone who doesn't care what you have but cares about what you are about internally. Nowadays when you do find someone who you think might be the one, they have already screwed so many or have been screwed over by so many others that they lose the true nature of love and no longer really know what love is. They think love is having this and having that but love comes from the inside not the outside."

From Mary: "I think good men tend to be attracted to and fall for women who aren't necessarily good for them, and vice versa. And simply put, many of the good ones are already taken."

From Kelly: "I am thirty-four years old, single, never been married, do not have any children, and I feel as though I never will have any of these things. Most of my friends who are either married or in relationships are unhappy, and I feel as though they just settled, but they look at me and say that I am afraid of commitment. Which is better, to be married and lonely or to be single and alone? Sometimes it all seems the same to me."

Is it better to be single and fulfilled or married? Fulfillment comes from personal accomplishments. It is not good to go through life looking for a husband or wife to fulfill you. You will be disappointed every time.

As a kid growing up in a single-parent home, I watched my mother marry for security. There are many women looking to do the same thing, and years later, they often end up angry or bitter because their needs aren't being met. That's why it's important to know what you want before you start looking for your good man or woman. Fulfillment comes from within. An unhappy person can ruin a happy one. I can't tell you how many times I've heard a woman say she left a man because he didn't make her happy. I met a woman once and when I saw her two years later, she was still leaving every man she met for lack of happiness. I finally asked her if she made the men happy.

She replied, "Men are only happy until the next woman comes along."

I said, "Well from now on you are going to be my home boy because you act the same way."

From Shauna: "Good men and good women have trouble connecting because some are tired of the rat race of dating, and they settle for what is in front of them. I also believe good men and women don't connect because we allow factors like finances, status, and physical attractiveness to drive our decision on with whom we are going to spend our time and our life. And lastly, I think some good men and women are so scared of making the wrong decision or choice that they don't dare to make one at all."

From Kenyatta: "I think men and women have trouble meeting because of all the bad men/bad women intercepting. On average, a good woman/man meets a bad man/woman before they meet a good one. If a bad man/woman comes in contact with a good woman/man they can hurt them in a way that could directly affect that individual's goodness. The bad man/woman can turn a person from good to bad by inflicting their negativity on them."

I know, sounds confusing, but Kenyatta is dead on. The devil is always busy, and he wants to turn all the good people over to his side, so he creates conflict and harm—ways for people to find "love" in the wrong places.

The flip side is being in the right place, but not finding anyone worthy of love.

Truthfully, even if you are in the right place—church, around trusted friends and family who introduce you—there are those who are not looking for a relationship or who are not capable of one. They want to play games. Mixing a good man or woman with someone who just wants to play mind games does nothing but bring hurt and pain.

For some people, they are looking for a certain mind-set. Determine what you're looking for, which you should know since you made your list in the "Define What You Want" chapter, then look for that in your potential partner. If you value your independence but your man doesn't, there could be problems.

A man doesn't have to be from the streets to appreciate a ride or die chick. It's basically a woman who has your back, no matter what. Loyalty is a powerful thing, and for many men, it can mean the difference between making a woman a permanent fixture or a passing thing.

During a recession, banks can go under due to bad acquisitions. It's the same thing with relationships. If your man or woman is a bad investment, at the first sign of a recession, the relationship will find itself in trouble.

KNOW YOURSELF

Even after you find your mate, you still have to work at maintaining the relationship.

I would implore you to learn what aggravates your mate. For Darren, it's too much physical contact.

"If you are constantly hanging on me or touching me too

much, I feel like you're clinging," he said. "Plus, I may have not decided what I want to do with you yet, so wait for me to initiate the public intimacy."

If your man doesn't want you holding his hand in public then he either has other women and doesn't want to be seen by one of them in an intimate position with you, or he's just not that into you.

Women often initiate the public intimacy to stake claim to their territory. It's a claim some women say men read too much into.

"I'm the type of woman who loves to show affection to the man I'm dating. I don't mind PDAs (public displays of affection) at all. My purpose isn't to impress others around me. It's more to let the one I adore know I appreciate him no matter where we are," says Carla, a thirty-nine-year-old teacher.

Looking for love is a complicated journey, but one all of us must take. There's one thing I've learned through the years, something that has made my lonely nights doable. It's the faith that my good woman is out there. I decided a long time ago to stop looking for her. I'm working on myself, and when God thinks I'm ready, He'll send her my way.

The same is true for most of us. My advice is to stop looking for your good man or good woman. Think about all the times you've looked in the past and how that ended. Matthew 6:33 says to seek first the kingdom of God and all these things shall be added unto you. My take on that is to walk in your purpose and you will find joy, even in your problems.

Once you experience that joy—that peace that surpasses all understanding—it's only then that your good man or woman will be found.

Obstacle 6:
Being Unequally Yoked

As a popular producer, I've met my share of women who think they're perfect for me. And some of them probably were and for various reasons (timing, baggage, etc.), I just passed them over. But the most confusing are the ones who claimed to be the woman of my dreams, yet they didn't have any goals or ambitions in life except to snag a man.

Think about it, and this applies to a lot of men I know. If I'm driven, don't you think I want a woman who matches my drive and ambition? Your helpmate should have his or her potential in motion.

Let's be real here. A man with means is not interested in acquisitions anymore. He wants a merger.

One of my grandmother's favorite Bible verses is Deuteronomy 22:10, which says, "Do not plow with an ox and a donkey yoked together." Growing up, I didn't quite get what she meant when she would tell that to various relatives. But then I watched a female friend marry a guy she just knew was her soul mate. She believed in hard work. He believed in handouts. She wanted children. He didn't. And the biggest obstacle, she believed in God. He didn't. They were all issues she thought she could work through, but after three long, agonizing years, she filed for divorce, telling me simply, "I had to realize we were too different."

They were unequally yoked, especially in their relationship with God, and therefore they were doomed from the start. What God is warning against—actually commanding against—in that Deuteronomy verse is any kind of bonded relationship with someone who is not in His reborn family. That certainly would refer to a believer marrying a nonbeliever. It can also be any serious romantic relationship. It could be a business partnership, even an intimate friendship. Those are danger zones for a child of God. In your core values, you're just heading in two different directions.

One of the most crucial things to building a successful relationship is making sure you're on the same page as your partner.

Women are nurturers, therefore they naturally want to help a person. That's why so many women are running around trying to fix the man they're with. That's what happened to one of the survey respondents, a twenty-five-year-old Miami woman who was in what she calls a bad, committed, on-again, off-again relationship for nine years.

"I want to leave but it's hard, and with the birth of my son two years ago it's gotten even harder to leave. I feel like I have wasted a good chunk of my life on this boy who can't be molded into a man. I am the breadwinner—always have been. I bring a lot to the table and never have my hand out asking for anything. I will be a pharmacist one day, and I want to find someone on my level, but the guys I come across are losers, jokes, pretenders, and phonies, and I tell myself better to deal with an old loser than a new loser. It has become clearly evident that the well of good men is running low and about to dry up."

This sister is doing what so many women are guilty of— the belief that a piece of man is better than no man at all, and a broken man can be fixed. In situations like this women may need to look at the fact that your man may not be broken, though. That just may be the way he is.

Most successful people want a mate who brings something to the table, not just someone who sits down and is ready to eat.

"I need to find someone who will complement me," Kenyatta said. "Someone who could bring something to the table and not just sit comfortably at my table. I had a lot going for myself, and men I would date seemed to think they could just get on board and join my team instead of us building or starting something together. And if I hear another 'I'm tryin' to start my own business,' I'll scream. If it was needing money from me to start their very own bootleg CDs and movies business or trying to buy a package from their neighborhood street pharmacist for distribution business, I have heard it all. It seemed every man I dated at some time or another was a 'bizness' man of some sort. It was like these men thought they were getting a five-star benefits plan with their membership, and I was getting nothing but a lot of broken promises and sometimes unrealistic dreams."

Added my friend Keith, "I had a woman rattle off the list of things she wanted in a man: a college degree, six figures, a legal occupation, a Christian, etc., and I'm looking at her like, 'Aren't you a stripper?' But she seriously felt like she could find that type of man, and I really wanted to tell her, if she did, did she really think he'd be attracted to her?"

Know this: an educated man does not necessarily want to be with an uneducated woman, or vice versa. It's just a matter of time before one person is intimidated or feels like the other thinks they are better. The reality is they are better—better educated.

Let me be clear, success is not measured by how much money you make at your job. It's about what you're doing with your life—a successful woman wants someone who adds to her life, not takes away from it.

Part of being equally yoked is doing an honest assessment of your qualities.

Men, stop lying about your financial situation. Know yourself, your bad purchasing habits, and what you can afford. If you tell a woman you have it under control, make sure you do. If she finds out you don't then out of survival she will kick into gear and get it done.

Before you start talking about all of the things you want in a mate, think about all of the things you are bringing to the table. Men say they want a good woman who is faithful, beautiful, independent, smart, who has not slept around, religious, and all that when they themselves have not been to church in years, go to clubs hoping to find their good woman, and have nothing to offer her. A woman with all those qualities would want and deserve a good-looking, religious, strong, intelligent man who has not slept around, right? I don't know too many of these kinds of women who would want anything less. Basically, you need to make sure what you want to get is what you're giving.

"I have not had a good date nor have I been asked out in a while by anyone I was interested in, but I will never stop believing there is someone out there for me," said my friend Ashleigh. "I believe there are good men out there. I just have not found the one for me. I believe we have to be self-aware. I'm not going to settle and put myself in a box for men nor will I date someone who I am not attracted to just to say I have a man. Essentially, I think good people have a hard time connecting with one another because they either settle, limit the possibilities by only dating a certain race/culture/age, or they don't align themselves with the things they want and value in a significant other. I haven't found my number one, but I am not going to give up and subscribe to the belief there are no good men. People must also balance what we want to get with what we are willing to give. If you have high standards then you may have to re-evaluate if those standards are realistic or superficial, and your willingness to compromise. If you have high standards, be sure you are living up to those standards as well."

My friend Sapphire sums it up best.

"As a single woman I've realized I should not be focused on what I'm looking for in a man, but what I have to offer as a woman," she said. "I should be able to live up to the same standards I set for the man in my life. For example, say I didn't work hard, was always going to the club, never paid my bills on time, but I'm praying to God for a man who is a hard worker, committed, and financially stable. He's probably praying to God not to find a woman like me."

The bottom line comes from the wise words of a sixty-three-year-old. "You must have a job or means of income, or be working toward that. I'm willing to work with you but not for you."

Obstacle 7:
The Cheating Heart

If I had a dime for every friend I had who told me he or she was giving up on love, I'd be a rich man. That was one of the saddest parts of sifting through the thousands of survey responses. Almost sixty percent of the single women said they had given up on finding a good man and had made peace with being single. Most reached that decision because they were tired of being cheated on.

I can't tell you the number of stories I've heard about a man either walking out on or cheating on a "good woman," leaving her brokenhearted and confused about what went wrong. I've also heard how he perpetrated like he was a good man long enough to make promises he never planned on keeping before his good woman kicked him out, often leaving behind a baby and a bunch of bad credit.

My friend Rene is adamant all men cheat. At some point in their relationship they cheat, she said. "And the sooner women recognize and accept that, the better off they'll be."

Rene believes the key is how he cheats.

"Is he disrespectful? Does he not have enough respect for you to cover his tracks? That's what you use to determine if you go or if you stay."

Personally, I think it's a ludicrous line of thinking, but Rene swears a lot of women feel that way. According to Menstuff, the national men's resource, she may not be too far off in her thinking because based on their statistics:

• Fifty to sixty percent of married men engage in extramarital sex.(Atwood & Schwartz, 2002, *Journal of Couple & Relationship Therapy*)

• Only forty-six percent of men believe online affairs are adultery. (DivorceMag)

• Affairs affect one of every 2.7 couples, according to counselor Janis Abrahms Spring, author of *After the Affair*.

• Psychiatrist Frank Pittman has found the divorce rate among those who married their lovers was seventy-five percent. The reasons for the high divorce rate include: guilt, expectations, a general distrust of marriage, and a distrust of the relationship.

• It is estimated that fifty-three percent of all people will have one or more affairs during their lifetime.

The fact is that human beings are not monogamous by nature. That means they cheat. Experts say a gut instinct is the most powerful indicator of a cheating lover. Adultery statistics state that eighty-five percent of women who feel their lover is cheating are correct. Fifty percent of men who feel their lover is cheating are right. The first clue is seldom obvious. Typically, it's a feeling that something is different. With whom you cheat also matters to a woman. She wants to know how she looks—was she prettier, younger, etc. She is searching for some evidence that perhaps the other woman has something she doesn't.

According to Annette Lawson, author of *Adultery*, "The various researchers arrive at a general consensus...suggesting that above one-quarter to about one-half of women have at least one lover after they are married. Married men probably still stray more often than married women—perhaps from fifty percent to sixty-five percent by the age of forty."

I believe men cheat for the thrill. They also cheat when they feel they are becoming too emotionally attached to a woman. It is the only way they know how to regain control of themselves.

THERE ARE THREE KINDS OF MEN:

The Just Do It Man—He sleeps with as many women as he can and brags about it. This is not only a badge of honor for him with his boys, but he feels it justifies his manhood.

The Just Don't Get Caught Man—He still sleeps with a

lot of women, but he is selective and you would never know because he is discreet.

The Just Don't Think About It Man—He has had enough sex to realize the differences and similarities between women, and he is no longer controlled by below-the-waistline desires.

The truth is all men possess all three qualities. We as humans constantly battle between reason and passion. In fact, your soul is oftentimes a battlefield, upon which your reason and your judgment wage war against your passion and your appetite. Some people call this the battle between the Flesh and the Spirit. This is why sometimes a person can be faithful and other times it seems an impossible task. It is when he is ruling his life by reason that man tends to be monogamous. However, when passion gets its opportunity, his insatiable appetite and sexual desires can move him toward infidelity. For reason, ruling alone, is a force confining; and passion, unattended, is a flame that burns to its own destruction. What determines whether you've found a good man is at what stage you catch him.

Timing is key. This is why you can date a man for five years and the subject of marriage never comes up, then a year after you break up with him he's married. You caught him during the wrong stage of his life. Dating a Just Do It or Just Don't Get Caught Man can cause a lot of women pain, especially if you're at a place where your biological clock is ticking and you feel you have to get married by a certain time.

I've seen women make it up in their minds they will be

married in a year, and many of them are, but I often wonder what they've sacrificed to reach that goal.

Have they accepted, like Rene, that all men cheat? Is that no longer a deal breaker—or have they reached the conclusion that a piece of a man is better than no man at all?

The fact remains, at some point in their lives, most men cheat. That's a sad reality, and for brothers like Leon, a thirty-two-year-old factory worker who doesn't cheat, it's a losing battle.

"I try to be faithful, never given my girl cause to believe I would cheat on her, yet and still she swears I have. And I haven't, but truthfully, there will come a point where I will. If you can't respect the one thing I pride myself on—being faithful—why bother?" he said.

Unfortunately, that's the reality many men adopt.

"We're expected to be dogs, so we're dogs," one guy said.

It's a cold, hard reality that many more women aren't buying.

"Men cheat because they want to have their cake and eat it too," said Angela, a forty-one-year-old nurse, "but let us do the same and all hell breaks loose."

That's another cold, hard reality. Men can dish it, but they can't take it.

"It's not right. It's not okay. But it is what it is," said one guy I talked to. "I cheated on my girlfriend five or six times, and she forgave me five or six times. The one time she did it, I couldn't get past it. I was crushed and heartbroken. When I cheated, it was all about sex, but for her to go sleep with someone, that meant there was a deeper connection, an emotional connection, and I couldn't get past that."

Men need to recognize sooner or later, your woman will get tired of your cheating ways. Take this story from one of the survey respondents. She's forgiven her husband several times for affairs. She has her reasons for staying, but now she no longer feels committed to her vows.

"I recently found myself attracted to another older man," she said. "I have felt like this for a year but would have never dreamed of acting on it. But I guess a woman gets tired of waiting for her man to do right. When she gets tired, curiosity comes into play and in my case, curiosity is about to lead me into the arms of another man."

She knows that despite what her husband has done, he'll never be able to cope with her doing the same.

"He wouldn't handle it well, the tables being turned. That's the bottom line. He simply can't handle when someone does to him what he did to them, just like a lot of guys. I'm at a point in this relationship that it simply no longer matters."

It's that tiredness that is causing a lot of women to simply give up.

"Every serious relationship I have had has ended in infidelity and manipulation on the male's behalf," said Ashleigh. "I just haven't found someone who can contribute to my life more than they take away from me. I look for someone who has dreams for himself and has faith in himself. I look for a man who I admire and trust so much I would be willing to submit to and follow. I don't consider every man I meet my boyfriend unless they have the potential to be my husband. I don't date to have sex or for fun. There is no point in me investing any intimate part of myself with a man who does not have these values or who is not worthy of my intimacy. I have given too much too many times, only to be left with nothing to show for it, and that is not how it should be."

Women, I have to be honest. You are wasting your time forgiving men over and over. If you catch your man cheating, he begs you to take him back and you do it very easily, chances are he will do it again. A man only values what he works for.

One of my married friends had an affair. I'd bet my right arm his cheating days are over because his wife sent him to hell and back before she forgave him. All he endured to get her back will make him think twice before he cheats again—he's gone from a Just Don't Get Caught Man to a Just Don't Think About It Man. When a man realizes what he could lose—I mean *really* lose, not empty threats he knows will never come to fruition—he will close down shop and change his ways. Hence, a man marrying the woman he started dating after you dumped him.

Developing trust is important. In some instances, trust is a precursor to love. Some would argue it's even more important because a lack of trust can destroy love. I can love you and not trust you at all. Successful relationships, though, must have both. No relationship will work without trust, even though a whole lot of people stay together and don't love each other.

Trust opens so many other doors. In most cases, it intertwines with love. If a woman doesn't trust you, then she can't submit to you. She is unsure you will protect her emotionally. All is not lost, however. There is some meaning behind the misery. Everyone can and should learn from failed relationships. Failure helps to prepare you for the successful relationships, so don't become discouraged by them. Instead, look at them as an opportunity to learn and grow—and in the case of finding your good man or good woman, someone else's loss might be your gain. Appreciate the foolishness of your past. Use it as a reminder, so as not to repeat any costly or embarrassing mistakes, but don't use them as weapons in your next relationship.

Obstacle 8:
Love

It might be strange to list love as an obstacle, but it's true. Sometimes we get so focused on finding love that it could be slapping us in the face and we wouldn't realize it. Love often makes common sense go out the window.

What's love got to do with it? That phrase was made famous by Tina Turner, a woman who admits she tried to love her man through the storm, but like Tina discovered, there comes a time when you must determine who you love more— him or yourself.

The answer should always be yourself. When you love yourself first, when you love yourself right, then you are opening yourself up to true love.

One of the first steps to getting on the right path of love is to be friends before you are lovers.

People aren't friends first anymore. We rush into relationships. We don't take the time to get to really know each other—we're too busy falling in love with the idea of love. I believe people should date for at least a year. The first six months is fun and games, the second six months is where you start to learn the truth about each other. What are that person's views and beliefs? What are their flaws, and have y'all laughed about them yet?

"Lovers have two components—the friendship and the sexual," said psychotherapist Vesta Callender "Friendships grow out of learning the other person's mind. This does take time and trust to establish a friendship. Sexual intimacy in relationships is very valued because it has a specialness and preciousness about it."

Callender said being truly friends and lovers is virtually in a class all its own.

"To have friendship and sexuality is special. Some people use the word *lovers* because it's a special name that conjures up mystical experiences," she noted. "Lovers almost sounds celestial. It's not so common that people have those experiences. That combination is very rare."

She believes some people steer clear of being more than friends with their close pals because they fear what's to come. As friends you're normally cool and in control, but if you become lovers, things will change.

"The one quality about love that frightens people is the element of mystical uncontrollability. To fall in love and to lose control of an element in your personality you're ordinarily in control of is frightening. When you fall in love, you may act out of character," maintained Callender.

Often men are afraid of love because love makes you do stupid things. A man knows when a woman is in love she will do just about anything. Well, a man doesn't want a woman to have that kind of power over him.

In a magazine interview, Dr. Larry Davis, professor of social work and psychology at Washington University, suggested people establish up front what they want in a relationship—friendship or romance.

"Don't go in playing like it's a romantic relationship but hoping it will be a friendship. If you want it to be romantic, play it this way," stated Dr. Davis.

He observed that some people believe just because they have a great friendship, they are destined to have an equally terrific romance. That's not always the case.

"Being friends won't guarantee there is ever a romance. We have more friends than romantic partners," cited Dr. Davis. "There's no guarantee romance will come out of a friendship, and there's no guarantee a friendship will come out of a romance. You can harm a friendship with sex because a friendship and a romantic relationship are different."

Added Dr. Davis, "Romance changes the nature of relationships because then there are more expectations. Sometimes it's a good idea not to act on feelings for friends. Women have more expectations. Men have to live up to the expectations."

In a friendship there is usually total honesty. When sex and love come in, the honesty may disappear, so there can be some drawbacks. Love makes demands on people that sometimes friendships don't. The expectations of what we have on someone we love are very different than the expectations we have on friends. Love involves a kind of mysticism where you don't tell everything. With good friends, you can talk about anything.

You can be emotionally vulnerable and not fear being judged or rejected.

"If you can get into the love affair and maintain the friendship," resolved Dr. Davis, "then you've got the greatest chance of longevity because you've got two things to carry it."

Notice I said friendship first. When relative strangers become lovers, it seems to be very difficult for them to learn to be friends while they're learning to be lovers. If they can manage to stay together long enough, they may have a chance to develop a friendship, but from what I've seen, it's a rare couple who can survive the ups and downs of a love relationship for any length of time without the strong foundation that friendship helps provide.

This can even be applied to sex. There's a big difference between being lovers and just having sex with someone. If you have sex with a friend, the friendship is often lost, although there are rare exceptions. However, if you have a friend who starts becoming a lover, you should recognize what's happening long before the sex ever happens. If friends who become lovers stop being lovers, the friendship will never be the same as it was, but if you were good friends and good lovers, it's very possible to maintain a friendship.

Jumping ahead to sex feels great in the short term, but it can distract a couple from actually getting to know each other on deeper, more intimate psychological levels. To me, sex at its best is an expression of intimacy and commitment to another person. Sex is an important part of adult play, couples should have fun exploring and experimenting in the bedroom.

Couples will almost always break up if sex is the only thing on which their relationship was built. Couples need to be compatible across physical, psychological, spiritual, and emotional realms, and it's difficult to assess those areas of compatibility when you're only having sex or rushing to have sex.

Behind infidelity and money problems, incompatibility is ranked as one of the most common reasons for divorce. In fact, it could be that a partner appears to be a soul mate in the courting process or in the first few years of a relationship when there is high physiological arousal related to passionate or sexual love, but the person ceases to be a "perfect partner" as the dynamics and expectations of the relationship change and the relationship alters to mature or companionate love—a feeling of deep attachment and friendship. These heartaches and headaches often can be avoided if people are friends before being lovers.

My advice: Rather than focusing on falling in love, focus on building your friendship with your good man or good woman.

Making Love Last

True love is a beautiful thing, and today we have some wonderful examples that give you a glimpse of what you can look forward to once you find your good man or good woman.

Barack and Michelle Obama are the epitome of genuine love. They show affection, support, and compassion. Granted, no one knows what goes on behind closed doors, but the couple is a refreshing sight. In an era of divorce, multiple marriages, and relationships that seem to fail more than they succeed, it's wonderful to see people in love—and making it.

No one knows how to make love stand the test of time like Ruby Dee and her late husband, Ossie Davis. Actors, activists, and partners for fifty years, the couple played their private love on a very public stage.

In the process they produced not only groundbreaking work on Broadway and in Hollywood, but three children and seven grandchildren, as well as millions of fans who have been changed by their love and art.

What keeps a couple together and still liking each other, not to mention loving each other, after fifty years? Prior to his death, Davis and his wife shared some of their wisdom in *With Ossie and Ruby: In This Life Together*. In that book, the couple revealed that while there are no standard answers, a sense of humor and good communication skills are high on the list of how to make a marriage work.

"Learn how to have a good argument and make it productive," Dee said. Also share the household duties.

Long before Women's Liberation, the two actors went through a tough time deciding to share the household chores so that each could continue to perform and write.

"Why does it take my life and your life to make your life?" Dee said she would ask Davis in numerous discussions on chores. "When a man marries he can drop half of his cursory responsibilities, the minutia of life, on his wife, while a woman has to double hers and maybe triple it when she has a family."

After Davis began to pitch in with their dinners and the diapers, things improved in their marriage, Dee said.

But there is a less than glamorous side to the happy couple, one that proves anything worthwhile requires work. The couple wrote candidly on the underside of married life. They discussed experiences with sexual temptations, abortion, miscarriage, and a short-lived experiment with open marriage, which they would not recommend to anyone today.

"Sometimes as the old adage says, you shall know the truth and the truth shall make you free," Davis said. "Not comfortable, not fat, not rich, but make you free."

The bottom line was their personal commitment to each other. "You see, what I always knew both intuitively and from a fact, was that I had come to the end of the search for the woman I wanted to be my wife, to be in love with, and to conduct marriage with for the rest of my life," Davis said.

"Ossie used to tell me," Dee said, "well, if you want to quit me, just make sure the guy knows that I'm coming too!"

The Davis' prove that a trustworthy relationship has weathered temptation, anger, jealousy, resentment, self-righteousness, and a little bit of selfishness. When you get over and get through that, then maybe you can see the light to love.

Other words of advice from couples who've made their marriage work includes that of seventy-two-year-old Eula Lee, who believes the biggest problem among young women is learning to be submissive.

"Women today hear that submissive word and they immediately tense up," she said, "but that doesn't mean be some kind of fool, or a doormat and follow your man blindly. It means the man is the head and the woman is to be his helpmate, but your man needs to be leading you like Christ led the church."

For years couples have been indoctrinated to believe relationships should be give-take. I beg to differ. A true relationship should be give-give, where each party desires to give to the other.

One of the major areas where many couples go wrong in the beginning of their relationship is in sacrificing things that mean the most. Most often, they're sacrificing and compromising just to appear non-confrontational. From the dozens of couples who are successfully making it work, one trait remains constant—couples should not sacrifice and compromise in a relationship, instead they should learn to acquire a desire to satisfy the other person out of their own free will.

One of my friends used to always go to basketball games with her boyfriend. The thing was, she absolutely hated basketball. She just went to make him happy. After a few months, it got old and started to feel like work. Her boyfriend couldn't understand why she no longer wanted to go to games with him, even going so far as to admit it was one of the things that attracted him to her. Needless to say, their relationship endured one problem after another until they finally broke up.

That leads to a big point my mother used to always say, "What you did to get him, you have to do to keep him."

So don't start doing things that don't come from the heart. You will have to find common ground, which is part of any relationship. The danger comes in when your real feelings emerge and they are contradictory to what you initially displayed.

If you're in a relationship that isn't going the way you'd like, ask yourself, what is wrong with the relationship we are in and how do we fix it? It's an assessment of where you are and where you're going.

And be wary of intentional sabotage. A young lady who worked for me was always having some man drama. I remember one time we were at a party following a show in another town and she saw her man talking to another woman. She watched the woman hand him something in a small bag, and she commenced to going off. Forget the crowds, the fans, everyone who was gathered at the after party. She went straight ghetto—cursing at him and the woman. It was absolutely embarrassing, and I was ready to fire her on the spot. But I didn't because once her boyfriend showed her what was in the bag—a diamond tennis bracelet he had bought for her—well, let's just say the pain in her eyes was enough for one day. But when he walked out of the party and her life, she shared with me how this wasn't the first time she'd lost it like that.

"Something's not right with him," she told me. "He's too good to me, and I know sooner or later he's going to break my heart."

The sad part was I knew this brother. He really was a good man, but she'd run him off, sabotaging her relationship because it just seemed too good to be true.

That intentional saboteur—where you have a seemingly perfect relationship and you're just looking and waiting for something to be wrong with the person—has ruined many a relationship.

If you still find yourself looking for your good man or woman, put this book down for a minute, run get a mirror (I'll wait)…now take a good look. Is there anything about you that is keeping your good man or woman at bay? Are you repeating negative patterns? Pursuing the wrong person?

Statistics show more women and men are divorcing in the Christian community than any other. The divorce rate is astronomical, and many relationships are doomed from the start because divorce is on the table before a couple even says "I do." Let's be real: Couples are saying "I do" but in their minds they are saying "I guess." It is too easy nowadays to give up on a relationship. If you think about the possibilities of divorce before you marry then chances are the marriage is not going to last.

I can't tell you how many comments I read on my message board about women who were taught by their mothers, "Baby, be able to take care of yourself." This suggests you can't depend on a man. If you go into a relationship feeling like you can't depend on a person, how can you ever expect it to work?

Some women will find a man with whom they can live, and they think because they can live with him, he is marriage material. A man, however, at least one who is being honest with himself, will only marry a woman he can't live without.

A lot of women go into relationships with their eyes closed and instead of dating the man, they start the relationship off by playing the role of the wife—they are cooking, cleaning, and sexing their man without benefit of marriage. But women need to leave something on which to build that relationship. That aggressive approach is taken advantage of by men initially, especially if he knows he is not ready for a commitment. The woman is scorned by the effect of this, and she then labels all men by what the other man has done. There's a domino effect afterward.

A friend of mine jokes her next husband is going to be smarter than her last one. She laughs, but she's serious. She doesn't think her marriage will last past ten years. She's doomed from the start.

That's a sad reality with so many relationships. Why? Perhaps it's because men don't know what women want and women don't know what men want. Perhaps it is because of infidelity, lack of communication, financial issues (not just lack of money even when wives earn more than the husband), interracial challenges, and unemployment issues…the list goes on. The bottom line is there are a growing number of relationships that end in destruction.

Deep inside every man there is a hero or a knight in shining armor. More than anything, he wants to succeed in serving and protecting the woman he loves. When he feels trusted, he is able to tap into this noble part of himself. He becomes more caring. When he doesn't feel trusted he loses some of his aliveness and energy, and after a while he can stop caring.

The following analogy from *Men are from Mars, Women are from Venus* perfectly illustrates my point.

Imagine a knight in shining armor traveling through the countryside. Suddenly he hears a woman crying out in distress. In an instant he comes alive. Urging his horse to gallop, he races to her castle where she is trapped by a dragon. The noble knight pulls out his sword and slays the dragon. As a result, he is lovingly received by the princess.

As the gates open he is welcomed and celebrated by the

family of the princess and the townspeople. He is invited to live in the town and is acknowledged as a hero. He and the princess fall in love.

A month later the noble knight goes off on another trip. On his way back, he hears his beloved princess crying out for help. Another dragon has attacked the castle. When the knight arrives he pulls out his sword to slay the dragon.

Before he swings, the princess cries out from the tower, "Don't use your sword, use this noose. It will work better."

She throws him the noose and motions to him instructions about how to use it. He hesitantly follows her instructions. He wraps it around the dragon's neck and then pulls hard. The dragon dies and everyone rejoices.

At the celebration dinner the knight feels he didn't really do anything. Somehow, because he used her noose and didn't use his sword, he doesn't quite feel worthy of the town's trust and admiration. After the event he is slightly depressed and forgets to shine his armor.

A month later he goes on yet another trip. As he leaves with his sword, the princess reminds him to be careful and tells him to take the noose. On his way home, he sees yet another dragon attacking the castle. This time he rushes forward with his sword but hesitates, thinking maybe he should use the noose. In that moment of hesitation, the dragon breathes fire and burns his right arm. In confusion he looks up and sees his princess waving from the castle window.

"Use the poison," she yells. "The noose doesn't work."

She throws him the poison, which he pours into the

dragon's mouth, and the dragon dies. Everyone rejoices and celebrates, but the knight feels ashamed.

A month later, he goes on another trip. As he leaves with his sword, the princess reminds him to be careful, and to bring the noose and the poison. He is annoyed by her suggestions but brings them just in case.

This time on his journey he hears another woman in distress. As he rushes to her call, his depression is lifted and he feels confident and alive. But as he draws his sword to slay the dragon, he again hesitates. He wonders, should I use my sword, the noose, or the poison? What would the princess say?

For a moment he is confused. But then he remembers how he felt before he knew the princess, back in the days when he only carried a sword. With a burst of renewed confidence he throws off the noose and poison and charges the dragon with his trusted sword. He slays the dragon and the townspeople rejoice.

The knight in shining armor never returned to his princess. He stayed in this new village and lived happily ever after. He eventually married, but only after making sure his new partner knew nothing about nooses and poisons.

Conclusion

So how do we develop an open and loving relationship? Well, you know I have to take it to the Bible. Confess and repent of all unloving thoughts, words, actions (Proverbs 28:13-14) and begin speaking open expressions of love by faith (Ephesians 4:15, 25, 29), and trust in God's power not your feelings or abilities (Philippians 1:6, 2:12-16, 4:13, 2 Peter 1:2-3), then find someone who loves you better than you love you. It will last a lifetime.

You can be open and loving by showing appreciation, spending quality time, giving encouragement, meeting needs, and bearing burdens.

We all have issues. The question is, can you tolerate mine and can I tolerate yours? You also have to be willing to do the work it requires to stay together, even consider counseling if necessary. It's not always easy, but very possible. I believe you can be the best-dressed man in a designer suit, great job, foreign sports car, and downtown loft apartment, but if you don't know how to communicate or how to stand up for your love against outside distractions, then you have a lot of work to do.

I believe there are a number of men and women out there who would make great husbands and wives—great mates, period—but they don't realize their potential. They're too hard on themselves. Once they've failed at one relationship, it seems they let negativity invade their space. Get up, shake it off, learn from your mistakes, and keep moving.

And above all else, never give up. People come into your life for a reason, season, or a lifetime. Until we learn what we're supposed to learn from the ones coming in for a reason or season, we'll never experience the love of a lifetime.

I say to both men and women learn to overcome the obstacles keeping you from your good man or good woman. Know yourself, define what you want and need in a relationship, look beyond looks, communicate openly and honestly, unpack all your baggage and don't let fear stand in the way of finding the love you so richly deserve.